P9-BYS-865

Life lessons from
our feline friends

Alison Davies

Illustrations by
Marion Lindsay

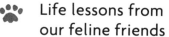

quadrille

FOREWORD

It's true that cats are a constant inspiration. Little did I realise when I adopted my two rescue cats Minnie and Honey, what magic they'd weave for this wordsmith. I knew I'd love them with a passion, but I've also learnt a great deal from both of them.

More recently when my beloved Minnie, aptly named because of her size, was attacked in the back garden by a dog, my true journey of self discovery began. With a 25% chance of survival, a ruptured abdomen and a broken spine, things did not look good – but Minnie is a fighter.

Against the odds and with lots of care, physiotherapy and prayers to the cat Goddess Bast, she got better.

She'll never be able to walk, but she has adapted her own unique and super speedy shuffle. She plays, climbs, and chases Honey, and together they have taught me that the power of love, a playful spirit and feline determination is a potent and unbeatable combination.

This book is for them and for every cat (and doting human) around the world. It's also for those less enamoured with our furry friends – if this is you, may a little feline charm work its way into your heart.

To one and all, be more cat and be happy!

CONTENTS

'WHAT GREATER GIFT THAN THE LOVE OF A CAT.'
CHARLES DICKENS

INTRODUCTION
CATS RULE

There is a bond between humans and cats that spans the ages. It's a relationship that stands the test of time. From the Ancient Egyptians who so revered their cats that when they died, the entire family shaved off their eyebrows as a mark of respect, to the cats of Malaysia who it's thought had the immense responsibility of transporting the souls of the dead to paradise.

The Japanese too have their Beckoning Cat, a potent symbol of luck. As the tale goes this canny feline raised its paw to a passing feudal lord, beckoning him into the temple just in time to save him from being struck by a lightning bolt. Replicas of this clever kitty are everywhere today, and thought to bring good fortune, success and happiness in all areas of life.

Who knows where the roots of our fascination with felines began, but one thing's for sure it continues with a passion. We watch them. We play with them. We make them part of our home and most importantly our heart. And we can also learn a lot from the way they deal with life. Their cattitude and ability to seize the day make them excellent examples of how to make the most of every moment; whether it's an impromptu game of chase the sock, or an opportune slice of roast chicken, our cats have it sorted.

They're flexible but also prepared to tread their own path and they recognise the importance of play and rest in equal quantities. These elements of the feline creed make them more than worthy of the title 'furry Zen master'.

This book reveals the NINE different traits that you can take on board to be more cat and live a happier, healthier and all-around 'feline fabulous' existence. With practical tips and exercises, interspersed with folklore and fun facts about our kitty gurus, there's something for everyone.

So sit back, relax and learn the art of BEING CAT.

'I HAVE LIVED WITH
SEVERAL ZEN MASTERS
– ALL OF THEM CATS.'
ECKHART TOLLE

1

CATFULNESS

LIVE IN THE MOMENT

Ever noticed how a cat can spend hours staring into space? Like a resting Buddha, our feline friends have learnt the secret of inner peace. They live in the moment, happy to clear the mind and take in their surroundings.

Look into a cat's eyes in these moments and you'll feel a WAVE OF TRANQUILLITY wash over you. It's no wonder the ancients believed you could see into the faerie other world by gazing into their peepers!

According to Old English folklore, the cat's eyes were not only the windows to its furry soul, but also a portal from which fey kings and queens could get a glimpse of our world.

Whether you believe the magical interpretation or not, one thing's certain; you can't disturb a cat when it's zoned out. It's virtually impossible to lift them from their stupor, unless you're prepared to brave the wrath of the claw. CATS MAKE MEDITATION LOOK EASY. They slip into a reflective state at the blink of an eye. This is because of their ability to dis-engage with what's going on around them. But don't be fooled; they're still very much aware of their surroundings and ready to pounce should the occasion arise. Like a skilled ninja they are masters of disguise; with the appearance of one so chilled out they might just topple off the table top, they are fully conscious and responsive.

So how do they do this and is it a super-power that humans can master? If you take the time to

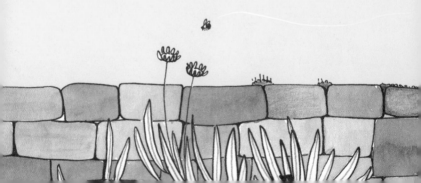

watch a cat in deep contemplation, you'll notice the way it fixes its eyes upon an object, making it the sole focus. As hunters they're primed for attack at any moment, which makes them keenly aware of their environment.

Whether they're sussing out a bird, a fly or the chipped paint on your window sill, they treat it with the same respect, fixing it under their hypnotic stare. A similar practice might render us cross-eyed, but this along with an ability to STOP AND TAKE EVERYTHING IN, is one of the reasons cats are Zen. Their conscious mind might be snoozing but their subconscious is gently appreciating the world, from a distance.

Some might call this '**MINDFULNESS**'; a popular and highly effective technique which improves health, well-being and peace of mind. Cats have been doing this since the beginning of time. This was one of the many reasons the Ancient Egyptians revered them so much.

They recognised the sacred power of this talent to embrace serenity, raising the humble moggy to a god-like status.

THE JOY OF CATFULNESS

It's a strange coincidence that the word catatonic, meaning in a stupor, should have 'cat' at its core. The truth is our clever felines maintain a fine balance between '**HIGHLY RELAXED**' and '**UBER ATTENTIVE**', something even experienced gurus struggle with.

Who better then, to give the low down on living 'in the moment' and experiencing **THE JOY OF HERE AND NOW**.

EXERCISE: ENHANCE CATFULNESS

STEP ONE
Find a comfy spot, preferably with a view, and make sure you won't be disturbed.

STEP TWO
Pick something that attracts your gaze, for example a flower, a tree or a building.

STEP THREE
Relax and look at the object you've chosen. Take in its appearance and let any thoughts and observations drift into your mind. If you get distracted don't worry, simply draw your attention back to the object.

STEP FOUR

Notice any outstanding features, for example is the flower moving, what kind of shape is it?

STEP FIVE

Engage your senses. How do you think it might feel to touch? Does it smell of anything or make a noise?

STEP SIX

Turn your attention to yourself. How do you feel in the moment, right now?

STEP SEVEN

Breathe and enjoy!

1

Appreciate the moment

Allow five minutes of every day to **JUST 'BE'**. Wherever you are, stop what you're doing and appreciate the moment. Consider all the good things that have happened so far, and give thanks. Remember cats appreciate everything from the breeze upon their face to the piece of fluff they find to play with behind the sofa. Let any negative thoughts go. Imagine tipping them into a dustbin and closing the lid on them for the rest of the day.

2

Focusing breath

When you feel stressed, **TAKE A MOMENT**. Focus
on your breathing, making inward breaths deeper
and outward breaths longer. Imagine a cat's eye
in the centre of your forehead. Feel it open to
absorb your surroundings. Rather than worrying
or forcing thoughts, just take notice of what you
see and feel and **LET IT PASS** through this eye and
out of the top of your head.

3

If you're feeling anxious, or that events are spiralling out of your control, press paws!

Spend five minutes massaging the centre of each palm with the thumb of the other hand, moving in a circular motion. **FOCUS** all your attention on how this feels. After a few minutes you'll feel less stressed, more relaxed and mentally alert – in other words **MORE CAT**!

4

Find your zen

When there's chaos all around and you need zen-like energy fast, **IMAGINE YOU'RE A CAT**. Assess the situation by taking a step back. See your eyes as giant portals and pretend you're looking out into the world from a position of safety. Note what you see without engaging your emotions. Rather than being in the situation, you're watching it from afar. This allows you to **BE IN THE MOMENT**, without letting it affect you. It will also help you be more objective and find effective resolutions.

5

Watch and learn

Whether you're a cat owner, lover or super fan, take some time out and study these gurus in action. Five minutes of **WATCHING A CAT MEDITATE** will de-stress you for the rest of the day.

Purrfect!

'A CAT, I AM SURE, COULD
WALK ON A CLOUD WITHOUT
COMING THROUGH.'

JULES VERNE

2

KITT-ABILITY

THE ART OF SQUEEZING
INTO ANY SPACE

CATS ARE ELASTIC. Like toothpaste they have the uncanny ability to not only squeeze into any space, but to slot therein as if it was made for them. No drawer, crevice or dusty corner is too small or out of bounds. They pour with ease, cramming themselves into slithers of air like furry acrobats.

The more challenging the scenario, the more they love it. To them, 'SQUEEZING' is an extreme sport, a must at the feline Olympics, ranking high along with the likes of the death-defying window leap or the stare-you-down competition.

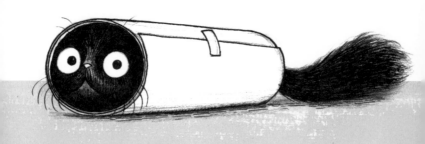

But what is it about our kitties that makes them such experts at balance and contortion, and why bother in the first place?

It's a fact that cats have ultra flexible spines, this is part of the reason they jump so well and always land on all fours. This coupled with a natural curiosity to not only know what's lurking in the space behind your computer, but to make it known that they are the master of this and every domain in their reach, is what fuels the fire.

Make no mistake, it's not just their physical litheness behind this super power. Their adaptable nature means that rather than admit defeat, they'll go to extra lengths to reach their goal. They understand the **POWER OF FLEXIBILITY** in all aspects of life. It may be impossible to go through something, but with a little ingenuity you can move around it and still be the cat that got the cream!

In medieval times cats were considered the cohorts of witches. Their lightness of being and ability to shift shape under the moonlight made them appear mystical in the eyes of our ancestors. We may not share these beliefs today, but we can still appreciate the supple dexterity with which our moggies operate. They are the ballerinas of the animal world, able to BEND AND FLEX when the situation demands. If we could adopt this same graceful ease, then our world would be less of a 'tense battle' and more of an 'artful dance'.

THE KEY TO KITT-ABILITY

Over the centuries humans have tried and failed to meet the exacting standards of their feline companions, but rather than spending precious time and energy caterwauling their issues, CLEVER CATS ADJUST. They have learned to alter their shape, appearance and general behaviour to adapt to the environment and make the most of it. By following suit and developing a flexible attitude, we can also find the 'win' in every situation.

EXERCISE:
TAP INTO YOUR
KITT-ABILITY

STEP ONE
Stand feet hip-width apart, shoulders relaxed, chin tilted slightly upwards.

STEP TWO
Place your hands on your hips and slowly bend forwards bringing your head towards your knees. Breathe deeply as you do this and keep your body relaxed.

STEP THREE
Slowly bring yourself back to a standing position. Take a breath and gently lean backwards with your hands on your hips until you feel a gentle stretch.

STEP FOUR
Return to the standing position.

STEP FIVE
Raise your hands up in front of you, arms extended until they're pointing towards the sky. Hold for a few seconds, then bring them down to your sides with a circular sweeping motion.

STEP SIX
Say, 'I am flexible in body and mind. I have learnt to adapt to ensure happiness and success in all things.'

BE MORE CAT – TIPS

1
Storyboard your problems

Draw a series of boxes like a comic strip to outline your problem or dilemma. Fill each box with words and pictures to describe your predicament until you reach the point of crisis, i.e. the point at which you're stuck. Now imagine it's a story and you are the author. If you were writing this tale, **HOW WOULD YOU LIKE IT TO END**? What steps would you take to reach the best solution?

Continue the storyboard, outlining your options. By putting the situation on paper and into a narrative structure you're able to be objective. You can see all the possible outcomes, which gives you a more **FLEXIBLE APPROACH**.

2

I can

Remove the words 'I can't' from your vocabulary.

Replace with 'I can' or if you prefer 'I cat'. Whenever you hear your inner voice speaking negatively, say '**STOP**' in your head and replace the negative statement with something positive. This will help you develop an open-minded, flexible approach and a **'CAT DO' ATTITUDE** in all aspects of your life.

3

Stretch like a cat

Use every opportunity to flex your limbs ready
for action. If you're sitting at a desk for most of
the day this is even more important. Cats may
have periods of inactivity but they always ensure
these are peppered with **STRETCHES AND TWISTS**,
to keep their muscles primed.

4

Shake things up!

Make small changes to your usual routine. Instead of taking your regular route to work, try something different. Imagine you're a cat exploring a new patch for the first time. Be **ADVENTUROUS** and **SPONTANEOUS**, so you might get off the bus/tube a stop earlier and take in your surroundings. Grab a coffee from somewhere new, or simply work your day differently by doing things at alternative times. The more you mix things up, the more accustomed you'll be to adapting when the need arises.

Be aware of how you hold your body and
what it can do for you. Imagine an invisible
thread travelling the length of your spine and
emerging from the top of your head. Feel it
gently tugging upwards, **KEEPING YOUR POSTURE
LIGHT** and graceful whilst your feet are anchored
to the floor helping to maintain balance.

'WAY DOWN DEEP, WE'RE ALL
MOTIVATED BY THE SAME
URGES. CATS HAVE THE
COURAGE TO LIVE BY THEM.'
JIM DAVIS

3

CATTITUDE

GO WILD

Cats don't care what others think about them.

As any owner will agree, there's something unpredictable about our furry cohorts. Expect the unexpected is a catchphrase which sums up the relationship between human and cat. Let's not forget these are inherently wild animals, domesticated on their terms.

We may think we have the upper hand, but that's a misconception on our part. CATS ARE IN CHARGE. They have learnt the power of the plaintive meow. Masters of manipulation, a wide-eyed pleading stare is all it takes to have us running for the tin opener and a tasty tuna feast. These intelligent creatures realised early on that they don't have to do their own dirty work, if they don't feel like it. Built-in hunters they may be, but every cat worth its salt knows there's no need to bark if you've got a dog!

Whether a cat chooses to hunt or to commandeer a helpful human, it will always have certain desires which it acts upon. This is not irresponsible in the cat world, it's simply the moggie creed. They have tried in vain to prime our hunting skills, going to such lengths as demonstrating and delivering prey to the doorstep, and for those humans who are really slow on the uptake, even at our feet. Dead or alive, these little parcels of love are both a gift and an example of FELINE PROWESS at its finest.

Cats follow their feral instincts. They have claws and they're not afraid to use them, but this is part of the reason we love them so much. They are free spirits. We respect, and in some cases envy this wild side.

In mythology, when the Norse goddess Freya plunders the skies looking for brave warrior souls to take to Valhalla, her chariot isn't pulled by horses as you'd expect. Instead she chooses the might of two enormous blue cats, a gift from the God Thor. These magical beings accompany her on her rounds and naturally feel quite at home on the battle plains.

When Old Tom, the cat in the famous British folk tale the King o' the Cats, hears the current King puss is dead, he doesn't think twice about leaving the comfort of his home and owner to take up the mantle of leader. On impulse he jumps up the chimney and into a new life.

Folklore makes it clear. Cats are the rock stars of the animal kingdom.

THE CAT ATTITUDE

Throwing caution to the wind might not be possible all the time, but as humans we can learn a lot from this 'SEIZE THE DAY' approach to life. Take a walk on the wild side and tap into your innate desires with this exercise.

EXERCISE: ENHANCE YOUR CATTITUDE

STEP ONE
Close your eyes and picture a rugged landscape with mountains and open plains, and the sun rising in the distance.

STEP TWO
Imagine you're standing in this place. You are the only living creature here. This is your domain.

STEP THREE
You run into the distance, quickly picking up speed until you're sprinting with power and force.

STEP FOUR

You reach what looks like the edge of a cliff,
there's nowhere to go but you're not afraid.
You take a deep breath and leap into the air.

STEP FIVE

The wind carries you, supporting your body.
You feel free and energised.

STEP SIX

You land gently and in one piece with the sun
on your back.

STEP SEVEN

Open your eyes and say, 'I embrace my
wild side, I have the freedom to do and be
whatever I choose.'

1

Unleash your wild side

The Egyptian cat goddess Bast protected women and cats; she also governed the realms of music and dance. It's easy to draw a parallel between movement and cats. They leap with wild abandonment and they're always up for fun and frolics. With this in mind, dancing is one of the best ways to **UNLEASH YOUR WILD SIDE**.

Stick on your favourite track and let your body move to the beat. Enjoy this freedom of movement and let the music lead you. If you devote five minutes of every day to dance, you'll start to feel free in other ways. You'll also find it easier to have fun and follow your heart.

Why not!

Make 'why not!' a part of your vocabulary.

Instead of quashing an idea or an invitation that you wouldn't normally accept, **BE BRAVE**. Say 'why not!' just once and see where it leads you. Cats are open to opportunity. Their spontaneous outlook makes the world a place of wonder and adventure.

This doesn't mean you have to stalk a mouse or harm any living creature. You can apply the hunting ethos to other aspects of your life. For example, make a list of five dreams or aspirations. Include a mix of small achievements and bigger life-changing goals. With each one write three things that you can do to help you move towards this goal. Each step brings you, the hunter, closer to your prey. For the next month make a point of taking a step towards each goal.

In some cases you might be able to go further and even **MAKE YOUR DREAM A REALITY**. Like the best feline hunters, fix your eye on the prey and slowly move towards it.

4

Be creative

When we use our imagination we're tapping into the psyche where our deepest wishes and desires reside. It's essential to acknowledge this part of the mind, even if you don't want to act on anything, as it brings balance and harmony to you as an individual.

Embrace this energy by **UNLEASHING YOUR INNER ARTIST**. If you've always fancied painting, take a class or get out and about and sketch the landscape. Feeling poetic? Turn your hand to writing. Keep a journal and note down thoughts and feelings in verse or narrative. Learn to play an instrument and record your musical creations. It doesn't matter what you choose to do, just give your imagination room to breathe.

5

This is a great way to start and end the day. In the morning think about everything you'd like to achieve, all the challenges ahead, and put all that energy into a mighty roar that **FILLS YOU WITH CONFIDENCE** for the rest of the day. In the evening, think of all the things you've achieved and any stresses or worries that might be bothering you. Take a deep breath and **ROAR IT** out of your system. Whether you've the tiniest meow or the growl of the lion king it's time to let it loose on the world.

'THE PROBLEM WITH CATS IS
THAT THEY GET THE SAME EXACT
LOOK WHETHER THEY SEE A
MOTH OR AN AXE-MURDERER.'

PAULA POUNDSTONE

4

CATTED
DETERMINATION

IF AT FIRST YOU DON'T SUCCEED...

According to a famous Zuni proverb, 'after dark, all cats are leopards'. This goes some way to explain their tenacious spirit. Inside every little cat there's a much larger feline powerhouse waiting to break free. This prowling predatory monster is the fire in the belly.

It's the spirit that can't be tamed, and the reason why our domestic moggies NEVER, *EVER*, GIVE UP. Whether attempting to climb a wall, jump on the top of the wardrobe, or scale the roof, once they have a goal in mind they'll do everything in their power to achieve it. Failure is not an option. And whilst an errant butterfly may distract them momentarily, ultimately they cannot be swayed from the cause.

CATS ARE NOT FOR TURNING.

An old folk tale claims that when Noah built the ark, it quickly became infested by rats. A despairing Noah prayed to God for a solution. The answer came the next day, when the lion during a wheezing fit sneezed from its nostrils two smaller cats. These feisty champions soon cleared the ark of rats, a task which must have at first appeared momentous.

As a result they were given the honour of leading the procession of animals on to dry land. Cats have never forgotten this. To this day they know they're worth it and this SELF BELIEF continues to spur them on. When other lesser mortals (and humans) would throw in the towel, the ever determined kitty draws on its resolve.

If in doubt, take a minute to watch any cat stalking a bird. It watches, it waits, it makes its move. More often than not it fails, because despite its many super-powers it cannot fly. Even though it clocks up numerous unsuccessful attempts it doesn't give up. Every day that follows it tries again with RENEWED HOPE, previous failures forgotten. It's ironic then that the word 'dogged', often partnered with determination, means 'having the qualities of a dog' or 'with a dog's persistence', when there is no other animal more resilient than a cat with a mission in mind.

COURAGE AND CATTINESS

If there's something you want in life, take heed
and follow the furry creed. You'll need a dollop
of courage and cattiness and the drive to give it
your best shot. If at first you don't succeed, do as
the proverb says – TRY, TRY, TRY AGAIN. You may
not reach your goal, but you'll have strived for
something and that, as any cool cat will tell you,
is empowering.

EXERCISE: ENHANCE 'CATTED' DETERMINATION

STEP ONE

Sit on the floor with your legs together and stretched out in front of you.

STEP TWO

Spend a couple of minutes focusing on the rise and fall of your chest as you breathe.

STEP THREE

Press your thighs into the ground, lengthen your body and take a deep breath in.

STEP FOUR

As you exhale say, 'I am determined', then lean forwards from the hips and clasp your ankles.

STEP FIVE

Gently press your head on your legs, without straining. Relax your breathing and hold this position for a couple of minutes.

STEP SIX

Gradually unfold your body and return to the sitting position.

STEP SEVEN

To finish, say out loud, 'I am determined'.

STEP EIGHT

Stand up and give your body a shake!

BE MORE CAT – TIPS

1

Remind yourself

When you feel like giving up spend a few minutes reminding yourself of all the wonderful things you've achieved in your life. Make a list and go right back to childhood. Simple things like growing up, going to school, getting a job can all be included. You've carved a life for yourself and done it with determination, but the journey isn't over yet! Get into the habit of **RECALLING AND CELEBRATING** your successes by spending a minute every evening reviewing all the amazing things you've done that day.

2 Jump for your dreams

Jump on the spot for five minutes.

Cats love jumping and they do it with ease and vigour. Follow suit and combine this energising activity with a powerful visualisation. Start small and build up the height of your jumps.

With every leap aim higher, stretching your arms up to the sky. Now picture whatever it is that you want, this could be a cherished goal, or success in any area of life. Imagine the key to achieving this is hanging in mid air. All you have to do is catch it. Every time you jump, imagine you're grasping the **KEY TO YOUR DREAMS**.

3

Tomorrow is a new day

If all else fails remember that tomorrow is a new day. You get another chance to go for it. **TREAT EVERY DAY AS AN EMPTY PAGE**. You create what goes on that page. Just like a cat embarking on a new adventure, you can choose to go anywhere and do anything.

Remember wise kitties get **OUT AND ABOUT**, preferring to throw themselves into each new day with optimism!

4

I can do this

Repeat the affirmation 'I can do this,' either out loud or in your head when facing any challenge. Say it with passion and feeling and for extra **OOMPH** say it in front of a mirror. The more you repeat the words, the more you'll start to believe that you can achieve anything.

5

Take a breather

There's a reason why cats let things distract them. They realise that sometimes you need to switch off and do something different to rejuvenate the senses. When things get on top of you or they just aren't working out, don't walk away, **TAKE A BREATHER**. Go for a change of scenery. Take a walk, or simply move into a new space and spend a minute breathing deeply. This will recharge your batteries, **CLEAR YOUR HEAD** and break the cycle of negative thinking.

'CATS SLEEP ANYWHERE, ANY
TABLE, ANY CHAIR, TOP OF
PIANO, WINDOW LEDGE, IN
THE MIDDLE, ON THE EDGE,
OPEN DRAWER, EMPTY SHOE,
ANYBODY'S LAP WILL DO.'

ELEANOR FARJEON

5

CAT NAPS
RULE

CAT NAPS RULE

Cats and sleep are a match made in heaven. Like cheese and biscuits, they're two pieces of a snuggly puzzle that fit. To watch these perfect bedfellows in action softens the hardest heart and inspires a comforting warmth inside.

But let's be clear, although cats snooze a lot
(up to sixteen hours a day in some cases), it's
not because they're lazy. Their **ADVENTUROUS
SPIRIT** means that when they're not sleeping,
they're usually up to something of value involving
strenuous amounts of activity and brain power.
To a cat sleep is not a luxury, it's an essential part
of their kitty toolkit. It allows them to operate at
full throttle the rest of the time.

The feline code is clear; you catch zzzzz's when you need to, which in effect means you are allowed to DOZE ANYWHERE! This amazing ability to shut down at the blink of a watchful eye, is something our kitties have perfected over the years. Their ancestors would have found beds in fields and barns, but cats today can be more creative. An empty shoe? A sumptuous cot to curl up in for a nap. A washing line? A make-shift hammock, high enough to be safe and provide stunning views of their kingdom below. The sock drawer? The element of sophistication with its own woolly mattress ready to mould to shape.

Cats, though regal and worthy of our respect, aren't proud when it comes to bedtime. They can make any space a peaceful haven.

Masters at the afternoon siesta, they carefully split their sleeping time, spending three-quarters in a gentle snooze-like state and the rest in full-on slumber. They recognise the POWER OF A GOOD CAT NAP. It also means that although they're deeply relaxed, they're still alert enough not to miss any action of interest! When they're in deep sleep mode they also dream, something we can tell from the rapidly twitching whiskers. Like humans, their brain takes this time to work through the issues of the day, like where that hole in the fence goes.

The difference between cats and humans is that cats embrace their napping time. Forty winks is ALWAYS guilt-free and part of their daily routine.

CATCHING A CAT NAP

Whilst we may not have time to sleep for nearly sixteen hours every day, we can learn some important lessons from our furry gurus. A cat nap to a human is like catnip to a cat; one small dose can perk us up for the rest of the day!

EXERCISE: PROMOTE DEEP RELAXATION WHILST AWAKE

STEP ONE
In your mind you're going to start counting backwards, from ten to zero. As you say each number you become more relaxed.

STEP TWO
As you say ten, you feel the space behind your eyes relax.

STEP THREE
As you say nine, you feel your mouth soften.

STEP FOUR
As you say eight, you notice your neck muscles loosen.

STEP FIVE
As you say seven, you feel your shoulders relax.

STEP SIX
As you say six, you feel your stomach soften.

STEP SEVEN
As you say five, your arm muscles relax.

STEP EIGHT
As you say four, the bottom of your back softens.

STEP NINE
As you say three, your legs gently relax.

STEP TEN
As you say two, your ankles flex.

STEP ELEVEN
As you say one, the muscles in your feet soften.

Breathe in the moment and let your body and mind embrace this snooze-like state for a few minutes.

1

Slow things down

When your mind is whirling, slow things down and restore calm by retraining your focus. Look at a spot on the floor or the wall in front of you. All you can see is this spot. Focus on the colour and **LET IT WASH OVER YOU**. Imagine being absorbed by the spot until you are no longer a part of the world, but separate, in your own space.

Give yourself a couple of minutes **PEACE** and, when you're ready, emerge from the spot and back into the real world.

2

Bedtime ritual

Get into a bedtime ritual. Like a cat, go for quality sleep. **SWITCH OFF** all your electrical devices (mobiles/iPads/laptops etc) at least an hour before bed.

Massage some lavender essential oil into your forehead, and also on the soles of your feet. Make sure your bedroom is well ventilated and dark enough for you to nod off. Keep the space **UNCLUTTERED** and **TRANQUIL**.

3

Natural rhythms

Learn to read your body's natural rhythms. Cats know the importance of rest. They listen to their body and accept that they need time to **RECUPERATE** and **RESTORE ENERGY LEVELS**. If you're feeling low and suffering with aches or pains, it's a sign that you need to relax and seek some balance in your life. Be still and pay attention to what your body is telling you.

4

Sleep

Before bed, say this positive affirmation nine times to encourage a **RESTFUL SLEEP**. 'I sleep soundly. Every inch of my body is relaxed and restored.'

5

Stretch it out

If you've ever watched a cat sleep, you'll know that every so often between snoozing it takes a long stretch, usually arching and lengthening its back in the process. This practice keeps limbs subtle and relaxes joints and muscles. **RELIEVE STRESS** and promote restful sleep by incorporating gentle movements into your day. Simple things like touching your toes, bending from side to side and rolling your shoulders will **KEEP YOU FLEXIBLE**, energised and also help to repair sore muscles.

'I HAVE STUDIED MANY
PHILOSOPHERS AND MANY
CATS. THE WISDOM OF CATS
IS INFINITELY SUPERIOR.'

HIPPOLYTE TAINE

6

WHISKER WISDOM

TAP INTO YOUR SIXTH SENSE

It's no surprise our ancestors from around the world were in awe of their kitty companions, believing them to have **SUPERNATURAL POWERS**. You only have to watch a cat when it gets that faraway glint to its eye, to sense that something beyond your power or understanding is going on. Cats have a mystical presence. They fix their gaze on the unseen, making it look like they can see ghosts. Whether they can or it's simply imagination is anyone's guess. One thing is certain, cats rely on their intuition. Their psychic super powers mean that they pick up on the slightest movement or noise, often sensing changes in atmosphere and the weather before we've reached for an umbrella.

According to popular folklore, when a cat washes its face and ears, rain is on the way, and if it should claw obsessively at the carpet then a windy day is forecast.

Sailors would use cats to **PREDICT THEIR FORTUNES**, believing that if the cat made lots of noise then it would be a challenging voyage, but if it was playful and sleepy then calm seas lay ahead.

It doesn't stop at weather predictions.

Cats were used around the world to divine the future. Early American settlers paid particular attention to their feline's washing habits. If their cat washed its face in front of several people in quick succession, the person it looked at first would soon be getting married.

Sneezing was also prophetic, with most cultures believing that a sneeze brought rain or a cash windfall.

Whether you believe superstition or prefer to take a scientific approach, cats have been the objects of our fascination for centuries. The combination of otherworldly grace and their often erratic behaviour makes them a puzzle we're still trying to solve. Having honed their INTUITIVE SKILLS over the years to sense impending danger, these enigmatic creatures do appear to be gifted with extra abilities.

Physically they can see in the dark, have twice as many smell-sensing receptors than humans and their whiskers pick up on vibrations in the air, helping them read the environment. This combined with a CALM SENSE of knowing that shines from their eyes, is enough to persuade us that they really are the cat's whiskers and wise little characters to boot!

WHISKER WISDOM

Whilst we're not blessed with the same physical attributes, we can develop intuitive skills to help us read people, situations and make the right decisions by watching and learning from the experts – our feline friends.

EXERCISE:
TAP INTO YOUR
INTUITION

STEP ONE
Find somewhere quiet to sit and light
a purple candle.

STEP TWO
Close your eyes and place both hands,
palm downwards, just above the navel
and below the breast bone.

STEP THREE
Breathe deeply and feel your body
expanding outwards.

STEP FOUR
Feel the warmth from your hands filling
your stomach.

STEP FIVE
Relax and let your mind wander. Be aware
of any thoughts or images that come into
your head.

STEP SIX
Open your eyes and note down anything
you can remember. Words, emotions, colours,
patterns and pictures are the language of
your intuition.

STEP SEVEN
Practise this exercise every day. If you have
a particular problem, make a point of
focusing on this, letting your mind come
up with the answers.

1

Open your third eye

This is the chakra associated with psychic
ability and intuition. It sits in the middle of your
forehead. To **ACTIVATE THIS BALL OF ENERGY**,
imagine a large amethyst-coloured cat's eye
situated there. Picture it opening fully, sending
a ray of golden light upwards. Ask to be blessed
with any intuitive insights.

2

Learn to read the signs

Like cats, we instinctively know when something is right for us. Sometimes it's just a warm feeling in the pit of our stomach, at other times we might feel a tingling sensation running up the spine. We also tend to know when something feels wrong; this can usually manifest in jittery sensations in the stomach, or tight knotting. Unfortunately, unlike cats we often fail to pick up on these signs. **KNOW HOW YOUR BODY REACTS** in different situations and tune into this whenever you can.

Remember your body is a barometer, it can sense positive and negative energy and it sends subtle messages to the brain to help you **MAKE THE RIGHT DECISIONS IN LIFE**.

3

At night the subconscious takes over from the conscious mind, which is why we often **WORK THROUGH PROBLEMS** and issues of the day as we sleep.

The subconscious mind is directly linked to your intuition, so it makes sense to tap into this powerhouse. Make a point of recording your dreams. Even if they seem nonsensical, consider every aspect from how you felt, to recurring words, images or symbols.

This will give you a clue to any intuitive insights. As you become more adept, you'll begin to **DEVELOP A KEY OF SIGNS AND SYMBOLS** and what they mean for you.

Take it a step further and ask for guidance before you go to sleep. Give any problems up to your subconscious mind.

4

Pay attention to yourself and others

It's easy to ignore advice or to gloss over evidence, even when it's staring you in the face. Our feline gurus wouldn't do this.

They're constantly aware of their environment, always searching for clues from tone of a voice, scent, stance and facial expression. Cats amalgamate all of this information before making a judgement about somebody. Follow suit and make a point of following expressions, tone and pitch of voice, and other body language clues when interacting. You'll develop a sense of empathy and find that your communications **FLOW WITH EASE.**

5

Balance and clarity

Carry a piece of tiger's eye in your pocket.
This lovely gem of a stone provides balance and
clarity and reminds you to trust your intuition
and **BE MORE CAT!**

'A CAT CAN BE TRUSTED TO
PURR WHEN SHE IS PLEASED,
WHICH IS MORE THAN CAN BE
SAID FOR HUMAN BEINGS.'
WILLIAM RALPH INGE

7

FIND
PURRFECTION

LEARN HOW TO PURR

A purring cat is a pleasure to behold. Whatever kind of day you're having, whatever problems you face, it can all be made better by this one sound. It resonates a calm warmth, a deep feeling of well-being that seems to pass between feline and human in a heartbeat. Often compared to smiling, the purr, in most cases, is a way of saying 'I'm content, I'm happy and I'm in a good place.'

But let's not forget cats are clever creatures. They've come to realise that 'THE PURR' is something we respond to. It's a noise we crave, making it a wonderful tool that can be used to get our attention when they're hungry or want our assistance. Being such bright felines, they also know how to adapt their purr for maximum effect. Scientists believe that by introducing a mewing sound which is not dissimilar to the cry of a human baby, they generate a swifter response. Coupled with pleading saucer-like eyes, it's an instant recipe for success, transforming cat owners into COO-ING devotees at the drop of a hat.

Not surprising then that the humble purr has other magical gifts. According to research, the dense vibrations which resonate between 20 – 140 Hz, have therapeutic properties. They promote the swift healing of broken bones, damaged ligaments and torn muscles in both humans and cats. It's also thought that the sound can reduce swelling and help to fight infection.

Feeling low? Spend some time with a purring cat, it will give you a MUCH NEEDED BOOST. Studies have even shown that cat owners are at less risk of a heart attack, by as much as 40%!

The purr truly is the cat's secret weapon, helping it to heal, charm and spread love in equal amounts. It's one of the ways our felines choose to express themselves, sharing feelings of joy liberally with anyone in the vicinity. As humans we often inhibit our emotions, limiting what we reveal to others, but cats aren't fussy. Nine lives out of ten, what you get is what you see and the HAPPINESS IS CONTAGIOUS.

FIND PURRFECTION

It doesn't matter where you live, it's a universal
truth that we all speak the language of the PURR.
It's time that we found this expression of joy
within ourselves and learnt to spread the warmth.
Lost for purrs? Look to the moggies of the world
for inspiration.

EXERCISE:
TO HELP YOU FIND
YOUR PURR!

STEP ONE
Stand with your feet hip-width apart, shoulders
relaxed and head tilted slightly upwards.

STEP TWO
Place a hand on your chest and spend a few
minutes breathing normally and quietening
your mind.

STEP THREE
Breathe in deeply to the count of four
slow beats.

STEP FOUR
Breathe out slowly and say, 'ahhhhhhh'; as you do this imagine you're unleashing your joy upon the world.

STEP FIVE
Repeat this process nine times, remembering to inhale for four beats and exhale the sound 'ahhhhhh', but make sure you get louder each time.

STEP SIX
Feel the vibration deep in your chest and the warmth as your lungs contract and stretch.

STEP SEVEN
When you're ready, draw the exercise to a close and finish with a positive statement like 'I purr with contentment and radiate joy!'

1

Compliment yourself and others

Cats aren't afraid to show their true feelings. Their purr lets us know that they're content. When we compliment someone we're doing exactly the same thing, we're showing them we're happy and that they're a big part of that **JOY**. Make a point of complimenting at least one person every day, this could be on the way they act, look or something they've done. Remember to compliment yourself too. Find one good thing about yourself and say it **OUT LOUD**!

2

Gratitude

Make 'THANK YOU' a natural part of your vocabulary. Give thanks to others where it's due and make a point of thanking the universe for all the wonderful blessings in your life, including the furry ones!

3

Find your theme tune

Find your theme tune and sing it loud! Imagine your life was being filmed, what song would be playing in the background? Pick something upbeat that makes you feel like smiling. Play it over in your head and when appropriate SING ALOUD at the top of your voice. Imagine that with every note you're not only SPREADING JOY, but attracting more of the same into your life. Whenever you feel down, recall your theme tune, hear it in your head and smile!

4

Smile, a lot

Unlike cats we can't make our laryngeal muscles twitch at super speed, but we can show our approval with a huge grin. Every morning stand in front of the mirror and **SMILE**, even if you don't feel like it. Exaggerate the expression and you'll soon find that your brain catches up and you start to feel happier. Once you've perfected the look, take it outside and make a point of smiling at other people. You'll find that just like a cat's **PURR**, it's contagious and can produce astounding results in every

walk

of life!

5

Acts of kindness

Share the love with an act of kindness. Do something thoughtful for someone else. Little things like holding the door open or carrying someone's shopping bags might not seem a lot, but they **MAKE A HUGE DIFFERENCE** and not only will you make someone's day, you'll feel all warm inside!

'I LOVE CATS BECAUSE
I ENJOY MY HOME; AND
LITTLE BY LITTLE, THEY
BECOME ITS VISIBLE SOUL.'
JEAN COCTEAU

8

FUR OF THE
MOMENT FUN

PLAY OFTEN!

Cats know how to have fun. They bring new meaning to the phrase 'LIFE AND SOUL OF THE PARTY'. From those first tentative steps as a tiny kitten, to tumbling and play fighting with their siblings, these balls of fluff are made to fool around. Play itself comes in many forms, from scaling the curtains and bouncing off cabinets, to an impromptu game of catch the slipper, with or without the foot in it! And it doesn't stop when they get older. Cats are constantly looking for new ways to amuse themselves. This is partly down to their NATURAL CURIOSITY, and partly an inbred hunting instinct, which means that everything and everyone is fair game.

The simple fact is our feline friends know the importance of LETTING GO every now and then. So what if they've a territory to patrol, or an interesting spot on the wallpaper to gaze at!

If the chance for some fun comes their way they grab it with all paws.

It's this spontaneous attitude that can get them into (and out of) all sorts of situations, but for the most part it brings excitement and JE NE SAIS QUOI to a cat's daily routine.

It's no wonder then that the Cheshire cat in the tale of *Alice in Wonderland* had that grin; he was most likely up to mischief and he didn't have a care in the world.

In literature old and new cats are portrayed as whimsical creatures, impulsive to the ends of their whiskers and also extremely clever.

Think *Puss in Boots*, a European fairy tale, written first in Italian by Giovanni Francesco Straparola. In this charming tale Puss gains wealth, power and the hand of the princess for his master, and all in a pair of stylish boots! The result of his hard work means that Puss spends his days living like a lord, and making his own amusement.

Dick Whittington, from the old English folk tale, also owed his fortune to a cat and its superb rat-catching skills. It seems for those of the feline persuasion quick intelligence and resourcefulness go hand in hand with the spur of the moment approach, and it works time and again.

FUR OF THE MOMENT FUN!

Whilst our furry friends may not (in most cases) bring instant fame and fortune, they do bless our lives with riches which cannot be measured. One of the most important things they teach us is how to kick back and have fun. If we do this regularly, we'll reduce the stress in our lives, FEEL HAPPIER and be MORE PRODUCTIVE and successful in the long run.

EXERCISE: PROMOTE PLAY IN EVERY AREA OF YOUR LIFE

STEP ONE

Before you begin make sure you're wearing comfortable loose clothing or exercise gear. Then clear a space at home, or if you prefer outside in your garden.

STEP TWO

Jump up and down lightly on the spot. Start small and put more energy into it as you go on.

STEP THREE
Increase the size of your jumps and throw your arms up in the air as you do this.

STEP FOUR
Imagine you're a small child jumping on a trampoline. Children, like cats, put everything into play, throwing limbs in every direction and having fun, so follow suit.

STEP FIVE
Whilst you're in the air throw some shapes. Have fun and let your silly side out!

STEP SIX
Steadily reduce the size and speed of your jumps, until you're ready to stop.

STEP SEVEN
Finish by saying, 'I embrace my playful nature every day!'

1

Find your inner chi

The Chinese believe that everything is made up of energy, which they call 'chi'.

Animals are full of chi and cats are the 'fur chi' masters of the world, because they know how to **BALANCE ENERGY** so they have plenty for play and new adventures. If you've a feline friend at home, they'll be able to show you the spots where the 'chi' is flowing nicely. These will be the places they feel most comfortable.

For happy, healthy cats and humans, keep your house free of clutter. This will provide your moggy with plenty of space to **HAVE FUN**, and will lower your stress levels, giving you more opportunity for human play!

2

The YES game

Develop playful positivity by playing the **'YES'** game. Whenever someone asks you to do something, even if it sounds scary or challenging, say **'YES!'** enthusiastically. We often limit ourselves because we believe we can't do things before we've even tried.

Silence your inner critic and believe in yourself by making a positive statement. Even if you struggle, at least you've tried something different, embraced your **PLAYFUL NATURE** and injected some excitement into your life. This in turn will give you a confidence boost and could lead to new adventures.

3

Cats are imbued with 'fire' energy or chi, so it's no surprise they're buzzing with kitty vitality. They **RECHARGE** this energy through deep sleep. The element of fire is associated with the colours red, amber and gold and according to research, using these colours around the home promotes an atmosphere of joy, success and excitement. Incorporate these shades in your decor.

Small changes using colourful accessories like cushions, throws, candles, vases and curtains make all the difference. You'll soon notice a spring in your step and the urge to have **MORE FUN!**

4

Take a decorative box of your choice and fill it with **PLAYFUL IDEAS**. These can be things you'd like to try, suggestions to make your day more enjoyable, even funny quotes, memories or jokes. Every day, dip into the box and draw out a piece of paper. If it's an idea or suggestion, try and include it in your routine. For example you might have written 'Dance like there's no-one watching'. So make sure you fit in a groove to your favourite tune at some point during the day.

Make sure to add something new to the box for every piece of paper you remove, so it's always full of **FRESH IDEAS** and **CHALLENGES**!

5

Cats understand the need to **ENJOY LIFE**.

They don't limit themselves when it comes to a good play session. They do what they need to do to be a happy kitty. Follow suit and make time for yourself.

Indulge in a pampering session, or treat yourself simply because **YOU'RE WONDERFUL!**

'IN ANCIENT TIMES CATS WERE
WORSHIPPED AS GODS; THEY
HAVE NOT FORGOTTEN THIS.'
TERRY PRATCHETT

9

MEOW POWER

TREAD YOUR OWN PATH

In life it can be hard to go against the grain, unless you're of a feline persuasion. Cats go their own way, always. Known for their independence, they may seek affection from time to time, but affirmation, PURRRLEASE! As any kitty worth her whiskers will tell you, 'you don't like what you see? That's your problem.' This can, to those who don't really understand the feline way, make them seem cold and fickle in their emotions. The truth is cats are so secure in their own fur they don't need anything else. They LOVE themselves and why wouldn't they?

Approval doesn't exist in Cat World, instead it's all about doing your thing (whatever that may be) and doing it in your own unique style. Moreover they expect to be thoroughly adored whilst doing it!

Listen carefully to the MEOW, which adult cats only use to communicate with humans, and you'll notice it's full of intonations. The rising meow sounding almost like a question – 'where's my tuna pretty please?' The sweet mew of a baby kitten could be for food and company, and a more general call to attention has both highs and lows in its melody.

Cats have learnt that the 'MEOW' has power. Like the purr it can be used to get what you want, and if you don't ask, you don't get!

MEOW POWER

Our moggies know how to express themselves, clearly, directly, and with a liberal dose of charm. They follow the heart and speak their truth at all times, something gurus around the world are continually striving for. To find your own voice, whether it's a meow or a roar, take inspiration from the cat world. Be true to yourself and tread your own path with confidence. Most importantly, love yourself, because you really are

Purrfect!

EXERCISE: FIND YOUR OWN VOICE

STEP ONE
Find a place that you won't be disturbed.
Stand feet hip-width apart, back straight
and shoulders relaxed.

STEP TWO
Slow down your breathing, taking time to
extend each breath in and out.

STEP THREE
With your fingertips curved into loose fists,
lightly tap a 'one – two' rhythm on your chest
and continue to breathe.

STEP FOUR
When you're ready, begin to hum a mmmmmm sound. Notice how it vibrates in your chest.

STEP FIVE
Increase the volume and if you feel like it, experiment by humming a tune.

STEP SIX
Hum as loud as you can and increase the tapping on your chest. Put all your energy into this and release any pent up emotions and stresses.

STEP SEVEN
Relax, smile and say, 'I embrace my true voice and express myself clearly every day'.

1

Make a list

Make a list of the things you love about yourself. **BE HONEST** and consider all your qualities, talents and the things that make you individual. If you're struggling, ask friends and family to help – other people will see and **APPRECIATE EVERYTHING** that's great about you, even if you can't. Pin the list on a notice board and read it every day. By regularly reminding yourself of all your best bits, you'll reinforce a sense of confidence and generally feel more positive, which in turn will help you tread

your
own
path.

2

Having trouble saying no, even when you don't want to do something?

THINK LIKE A CAT and dig in your claws. Practise saying no firmly by screwing both hands into tight fists and saying 'no thank you', or 'no I don't want to do that.' If it helps, do this in front of a mirror. When you find yourself in a situation where you're nervous about saying no, simply ball up your fists, **TAKE A DEEP BREATH** and speak your truth. The physical act of digging in your claws will help you remember how to say no politely and firmly just like you've practised.

3

Seek out new adventures

Finding the confidence to **FOLLOW YOUR HEART** takes small steps. Like a cat exploring new territory, we don't know what's around the corner and that's what makes it exciting. Purposely make a point of exploring your area.

Go for a walk somewhere you've never been and don't worry if you get lost. You'll always **FIND YOUR WAY**, but the experience will open your eyes and make you see that following your own path, however different, can be liberating.

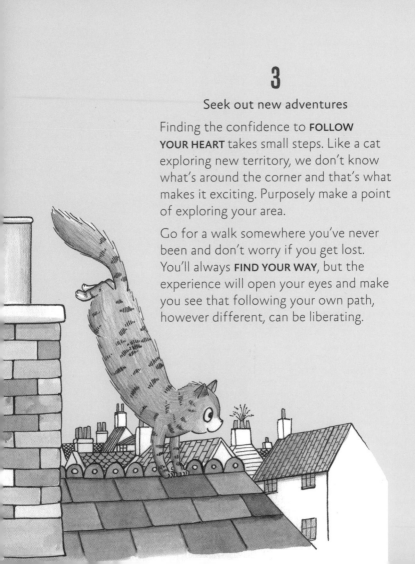

4

Sense of self

Invest in a piece of Dragon's Eye. This colourful stone is thought to enhance your sense of self, provide a **CONFIDENCE BOOST** and also increase vitality. Wear or carry to *put* a spring in your step!

5

Feline decor

Make your home a kitty haven. Include images of cats in your decor, so go for tablecloths, wall paper, cushions, pictures and ornaments with a feline feel. When we surround ourselves with images of our furry friends, we're reminded of their **INDIVIDUALITY** and **SPIRIT**, which in turn makes us more likely to adopt these qualities.

Publishing Director Sarah Lavelle
Creative Director Helen Lewis
Commissioning Editor Lisa Pendreigh
Editor Harriet Butt
Designer Nicola Ellis
Illustrator Marion Lindsay
Production Tom Moore, Vincent Smith

First published in 2017 by Quadrille,
an imprint of Hardie Grant Publishing

Quadrille
52–54 Southwark Street
London SE1 1UN
quadrille.com

Reprinted in 2017 (twice), 2018
10 9 8 7 6 5 4

Text © 2017 Alison Davies
Illustrations © 2017 Marion Lindsay
Design and layout © 2017 Quadrille Publishing

Cataloguing in Publication Data: a catalogue
record for this book is available from the
British Library.

ISBN: 978 184949 952 1
Printed in China